England in cameracolour
Cotswolds
and Shakespeare Country

England in cameracolour
Cotswolds
and Shakespeare Country

Photographs by F. A. H. BLOEMENDAL

Text by ALAN HOLLINGSWORTH

LONDON
TOWN & COUNTY BOOKS
IAN ALLAN GROUP

First published 1980
Third impression 1988

ISBN 0 7110 0920 1

© Ian Allan Ltd 1979

Published by Ian Allan Ltd, Shepperton, Surrey;
and printed in Italy by
Graphische Betriebe Athesia, Bolzano

Introduction

The Cotswold hills overlook the quiet vale of Shakespeare's Avon and the whole area is close to England's heartland. It is close, too, to the heart of every Englishman not just because it contains the birthplace of the greatest of English poets but because it also epitomises all that is best in English landscape and the English tradition in rural building. If there ever was a rustic golden age of 'Merrie England', one feels that it was here – and looking at many of the villages and market towns, here only yesterday. In the pages that follow, the distinguished Dutch landscape photographer, F. A. H. Bloemendal, has painted a portrait of this superb corner of England that largely speaks for itself. He has successfully captured not just the image of the hills, the streams, the woods, the villages and the buildings that go to make up landscape but also by his choice of subject, that sense of atmosphere and personality that distinguishes the work of the true artist.

A map of the area is at each end-paper and the rough order followed by the photographs is that of an imaginary journey from Broadway northwards to Stratford and Warwick then southwards again through the Cotswolds to Burford, then westwards via Cirencester and Tetbury to Dursley, thence northwestwards along the 'Edge' back to Broadway.

The focal point of the whole area is Stratford-on-Avon and its associations with William Shakespeare who was born there, tradition has it, on 23 April 1564. He lived in Stratford until the late 1580s when he went to London and became first an actor and then a playright. Of his early life in Stratford, little is known. It is generally accepted that he attended the grammar school and sat in the long classroom over the Guild Hall (see page 28). It is known that in 1582 he married Anne Hathaway who was eight years his senior. She came from the nearby village of Shottery and, as most of the English-speaking world knows, her cottage still stands today (see page 34). Shakespeare published his first major poem *Venus and Adonis* in 1593 and thereafter rose steadily in esteem and prosperity until the end of the century. In 1597 he bought New Place next to the house which carries the name today but of which nothing remains except the garden (see page 30). Shakespeare retired from London in 1610 and returned to Stratford where he died on 23 April 1616.

What is nowadays called the 'Shakespeare Country' has no definite bounds but is generally accepted as being the vale of the Avon running roughly from Bidford-on-Avon through Stratford to Warwick and Leamington and comprising the rural southern half of the ancient county of Warwick. Apart from its Shakespearean associations, this part of Warwickshire is particularly rich in timber-framed houses which have survived from Elizabethan and Jacobean periods and range from 'great houses' to humble cottages. These buildings together with many others from the Georgian period set against the background of one of the most peaceful of English rivers, fringed with willows, its banks alight with wild flowers, flowing gently through tranquil English meadows, add immensely to the appeal of an area already attractive because of its place in history.

In areas like Warwickshire, with its numerous oak trees and plentiful clay, timber-framed houses were built from very early times until well into the 19th century – the typical 'Tudor' cottage of which many examples will be found in the pages that follow. The earlier and more primitive types had what is called 'cruck' framing in which pairs of long curved beams were leant together to form a kind of arch which supported both roof and walls. (These crucks can sometimes been seen at the end walls of such buildings, one such is Anne Hathaway's cottage (see page 34).) A later form involved the creation of a 'box-frame' of timbers with square panels and diagonal braces but in the Stratford area there are many examples of hybrid cruck and box-frame types. The panels between the timber frames were usually filled with 'wattle' – a screen of interwoven willow or hazel wands coated (ie 'daubed') with a mixture of clay, dung, horsehair which was allowed to dry and was then finished off with a coat of plaster inside and out. Other materials were also used for the in-filling: tiles, slate and thin stone slabs but the usual alternative in the Shakespeare country is brick – the proper name is 'brick-nogging' – which is more appropriate to the square panels between the timber often found in the area.

5

One common feature of timber houses is the overhanging upper storey known as a 'jetty' where the floor beams were cantilevered to provide a base for the walls of the upper storey. Originally introduced as a means of saving space — and expensive timber — in restricted town sites, jettied construction spread rapidly as a fashion. Lord Leycester's Hospital (see page 36), for example, is 'jettied'.

Timber was always expensive and old timbers were frequently re-used and this explains the number of joints, slots and peg-holes which can often be seen on posts and beams internally and externally. Timbers too — especially oak timbers — tended to be left in their natural state. The naturally-weathered brown of the frames and the yellowed tone of the in-filling as in the Stratford Guildhall and Grammar school, Anne Hathaway's Cottage and Lord Leycester's Hospital (see pages 28, 34, 36) are hence more authentic than those buildings where a later age has tarred the timbers black and white-washed the infilling as in Oken's House in Warwick (see page 38).

Not all the ancient buildings of the Shakespeare country are of timber-framed construction and the most notable exceptions are the great red sandstone castles of Warwick, Kenilworth and Maxstoke. But such stone was rarely suitable or readily available for the simpler domestic buildings and timber framing under a thatched roof was the general rule. In sharp contrast, limestone characterises much of the landscape and buildings of the Cotswolds only a few miles further south.

The particular Jurassic limestone of the Cotswolds is composed of small rounded grains of calcium carbonate formed millions of years ago from the broken and powdered shells of primitive organisms — corals, sea-lilies and molluscs — which lived in some primeval tropical sea. These grains are pressed together like the roe of a fish and hence have the name 'oolite', meaning egg-stone. It is a soft rock which, like other limestones, is soluble in weak acids and rainwater is a dilute carbonic acid. The Cotswolds are well watered by the Atlantic sou'westers and thousands of years of weathering have given them their gracefully smooth shapes and contours. Nowhere are there angular or lumpish hills, even in the south west where there is more folding and slopes are steeper. Only in a few places can the basic rock of the Cotswolds be seen naturally on the surface — apart from numerous quarries — but it flowers above the surface in mansion, farm-house, cottage and ancient barn like a natural growth from the mother rock below.

The lower and older stratum of Cotswold limestone called Inferior Oolite is tilted upwards at its western edge where it forms the Cotswold escarpment and the higher hills, rising in places to about 1,000ft. As it dips eastwards into Oxfordshire, the Inferior Oolite runs under the Great Oolite, a newer sandy limestone with smaller grains which contains tiny pieces of white mica that make it fissile and easy to split into thin layers. In general it is the Inferior Oolite which provides the building stone and the Great Oolite the characteristic Cotswold stone tiles. What the geologist calls the 'regular bedding plane' of the Inferior Oolite — literally natural shelves of stone broken vertically at intervals — have given it the generic title of 'freestone' among quarrymen because it is so convenient to handle and work. The stone varies in colour from cream to brown depending upon the amount of iron mineral called lumanite in the stratum. The greater depth from which the stone is quarried the deeper is the yellow but as it dries out it turns to a light yellowish brown like honey. Inferior Oolite is easily worked when freshly quarried and is used for a variety of architectural features from door and window frames to fireplaces and mouldings and decorations of all kinds. After exposure, however, the stone hardens and becomes extremely durable and is much in demand nowadays for restoration work on churches.

Roofing tiles of Cotswold stone come from special surface quarries — Sevenhampton Common near Andoversford is a well-known site although the industry has now disappeared from the area. The tilestones come in two main types: 'presents' which are found near the surface virtually ready for use, and 'pendle' which had to be dug out in thick slabs from underground. Slabs of pendle were kept wet with their natural water until the winter when they were exposed until the frost split them into thin tiles. 'Getters' got tiles out of the ground and 'slatters' were the men who made them unto usable slates; tilers then laid them on the roofs. Tilers too had their own time-honoured vocabulary — tiles were laid with small ones – 'cocks' or 'tants' – under the ridge stones, ones of increasing size – 'becks', 'batchelors' and 'longs' – beneath them with 'cussems' – up to two feet wide and weighing as much as 50lb – running along the eaves.

Building stone from beds of Oolite is found at many places along the long ridge of Jurassic limestone which runs from Dorset to Lincolnshire. What gives the Cotswolds their particular distinction is the quality of the buildings found there, from humble barns to magnificent churches, and the manner in which they blend so harmoniously with the landscape. The colour of the building stone plays its part but there is also a traditional style of architecture which has its origins in Tudor times and continues to exert its influence still – it is usually called the 'Cotswold vernacular'. In essence it is Elizabethan but its very suitability to local materials and local conditions ensured its survival until as late as the early 18th century.

Not all Cotswold houses show all the main characteristics of the 'Cotswold vernacular' but it is unusual not to find at least one or two features even in houses built in a radically different tradition like the Neo-Classical style beloved of the Georgians. Perhaps the most pervasive feature is the stone-tiled roof with its graded tiles and though the geographic boundaries of the Cotswold area may not be well defined, many people accept that the prevalence of stone tiling denotes 'the Cotswolds' more surely than any map. These oolite tiles tend to absorb water and for this reason they are set on high pitched roofs to drain well. High pitched roofs inevitably call for gables or dormers bearing windows to admit light to the roof space, and these too have high-pitched roofs. Often there is some form of coping at the gable end and quite frequently, a decorative finish or, on the face of the gable, a niche containing a carving.

Two main types of stonewalling are to be found in Cotswold houses: ashlar and rubble. Ashlar occurs mostly in the bigger houses where carefully dressed 'freestones' are laid in regular courses. Ashlar can always be recognised by the smooth facing, accurate blocks and, above all, the thin almost mortarless joints. Rubble masonry is, as its title implies, the use of random uncut stone blocks of various shapes and sizes laid with thick mortar joints. A variety often found in the Cotswolds where the stone splits regularly, is 'coursed' rubble – blocks are selected to bed horizontally.

Next to stone-tiling and stone walling, the other great Cotswold characteristic is the mullioned window with its drip mould. Mullions are the vertical stone uprights that divide windows into individual 'lights' – two, three and four are the ones most prevalent – and they owe their origin to the Middle Ages when many churches and monastic buildings were erected. Following Henry VIII's Dissolution of the Monasteries, the many stone-masons and other craftsmen employed in their upkeep found employment in building houses as the wool trade brought increasing prosperity to the area. They were the founders of the Cotswold vernacular and the mullioned window is one of their hallmarks. So too is the characteristic drip mould – the narrow stone projection just above a door or window designed to throw rainwater clear. These tend to be 'hood-moulds' – shaped like a square bracket. Very frequently Cotswold mullions are glazed with leaded lights and it is not unusual in older houses to find individual lights divided horizontally by transoms and with cusped or arched heads to add further to their ecclesiastical appearance. Another church-like feature is the solid stone doorway with its traditional four-centred arch often with carved spandrels over it. Chimneys tend to be tall and often in clusters, well decorated and capped. Finally, the frustrated artistic aspiration of these monastery masons – and their descendants – found expression in a host of decorative carvings from finials to frescoes.

The last photograph in the book is of the celebrated tower on Broadway Hill which has a room devoted to William Morris who was the actual discoverer of the Cotswold vernacular style, although the name itself came later. He described his own Cotswold house, Kelmscott Manor near Lechlade, as: 'the type of the pleasant places of the Earth, and of the homes of the harmless simple people not overwhelmed by the intricacies of life.'

This then is the heart of England . . . .

Alan Hollingsworth

Court House, Bury End, Broadway, Worcestershire. The gateway shown here is all that remains of the original manor house of the old village of 'Brod Way'. With its stone-tiling, steep gables, tall chimney stacks, precisely-moulded mullions and door-heads, its decorative carving and above all its mellow honey-coloured stone, it is an excellent example of the local architectural tradition that adds so much to the character and appeal of the Cotswold area. Built in Elizabethan times it was once the home of the Sheldons, Broadway's last great land-owning family many of whom lie in the adjoining Norman church dedicated to St Edburgh, grand-daughter of King Alfred the Great, who died in 960 AD and whose relics were enshrined in Pershore Abbey which owned Broadway until 1539.

8

The Green, Broadway. Broadway, Brod Way or Brodey has for centuries been a staging post on the long road from Wales via Worcester and Oxford to London. The main road has not always passed through the village High Street — until about 1650 it ran through the West End of the village and up to Snowshill — but the High Street has always been broad and it is generally accepted that this explains the name. But Broadway has for centuries been a centre for travellers to take rest and refreshment, just as it is today. The Broadway Hotel shown opposite, for example, was once the village bakery but it also had earlier connections with the nearby Abbot's Grange where, before the Dissolution of the Monasteries in 1539, monks and nuns from the Abbey of Pershore were sent for physical and spiritual restoration. Part of the hotel is said to be haunted by the ghost of a weeping nun but who she was and why she weeps, none can now tell.

High Street, Broadway. Broadway's High Street is not only broad, it is also lined with superb chesnut trees like the ones depicted here. At one time – until 1862 – there were two streams running down the main street, one on either side which may account for the width of the street and also its curving path up the hill. The hotel in the centre of the picture is the celebrated Lygon Arms which was first built at the end of the 15th century. It was known as the White Hart until 1820 and it is believed that both Cromwell and King Charles I may – on separate occasions – have stayed there.

Chipping Campden, Gloucestershire. One of the most famous and beautiful of all Cotswold villages, Chipping Campden has been credited with having 'the most beautiful village street in England'. It takes its name from the Old English word 'ceiping' meaning a market and was for nearly 200 years a prosperous centre of the Cotswold wool trade. Evidence of this prosperity is the magnificent church, shown in the centre of the picture, which was built in the 14th and 15th centuries with some older Norman work still to be seen. The stately tower is 120ft tall, and the church itself has walls five feet thick and is longer from east to west than the tower is high. Behind the town is Dover's Hill where once the annual 'Cotswold Olympicks' were held. Lasting for more than 200 years, they comprised horse racing, hare coursing, cockfighting and the 'manly' contest of shin-kicking. The Games degenerated into rowdyism and came to an end in 1851 but have recently been revived.

14

Chipping Campden Market Hall. This arcaded Jacobean market hall affords a favourite place from which to admire the celebrated High Street. It was built in 1627 by the first Lord Campden, Sir Baptist Hicks, a famous merchant of Charles I's day who gave new life to Campden after it had begun to decay following the ending of the wool trade. (The Hicks coat of arms is under one of the gables.) Now the property of the National Trust, the Market Hall was once threatened with demolition and transport to the United States. It was saved by the intervention of the Campden Trust which has been largely responsible for preserving the architectural beauty of the town.

16

Chipping Campden – Almshouses, Church Tower and the Gateway to Campden House. Another of the benefactions of Sir Baptist Hicks was the terrace of Almshouses on the left of the picture. Although they were modernised in 1959, these superb houses, built in 1612, have been described as 'the crowning achievement of the domestic Cotswold style'. The church tower was built in the early 15th century and has Cotswold diagonal buttresses and 12 pinnacles. Beneath the tower there is to be found a collection of magnificent medieval embroidery and in the south chapel some beautifully sculptured memorials on the tombs of the Hicks family. Another memorial to them is to be found in the gatehouse on the right of the church – all that remains of Campden House which was deliberately put to the flames by Prince Rupert's Cavaliers to prevent it falling into Cromwell's hands.

Hidcote Manor Gardens, near Chipping Campden, Gloucestershire. One of the most beautiful gardens of the 20th century, Hidcote Manor gardens were created by an American officer, Major Lawrence Johnston, who acquired the house, a few walls, the cedar of Lebanon on the right of the picture, and a clump of beech trees in 1905. The whole garden now covers 11 acres and is divided by walls or hedges into numerous separate small gardens, each having a distinctive colour scheme and each planted with a different selection of shrubs and flowers to provide a display from spring to autumn. Many rare plants are to be found here – a unique old double tulip, for example, and lavender, hypericum and verbena all bearing the Hidcote name. Most appropriately perhaps is the rose which bears Lawrence Johnston's.

Weston-sub-Edge, Gloucestershire. As its name implies, Weston-sub-Edge lies under the northernmost edge of the Cotswold escarpment beneath Dover's Hill and close to the Roman Ryknield Street which ran from Alcester to Stow-in-the-Wold. An out-of-the-way village, it has many fine 17th century houses like the one shown here, a number grouped round a square and boasting as this one does some excellent examples of the topiarist's art. The hybrid construction is interesting — part Cotswold stone and part half-timbering — one of the many examples to be found where the Cotswolds begin to give way to the Vale of Evesham and Gloucestershire to Warwickshire.

22

Bidford-on-Avon, Warwickshire. Where the Roman Ryknield Street — or Buckle Street as it was later known — crosses the Avon and enters the true 'Shakespeare Country'. The bridge which has eight arches was old even in Shakespeare's day and is renowned for the view it affords of quiet waters and the distant prospect of the Cotswolds. A familiar term is 'Drunken Bidford' — a reference to the traditional tale that Shakespeare and his companions had a drinking bout with the 'Bidford Society of Sippers' and lost, falling, dead-drunk, under a crab-apple tree until they revived. The site of the contest is said to be the Falcon Inn on the north side of the church.

Welford-on-Avon, Warwickshire. Another of the charming villages that Shakespeare must have known, Welford has a number of features that go back to his time — an ancient mill and an even older church with a register which records the flooding of the Avon in 1588 caused by the same gale that wrecked the Spanish Armada. The date of these cottages is uncertain — they have clearly been much restored — but the thatch and the timber-framing is in the Warwickshire rather than the Cotswold vernacular.

Church Street, Stratford-on-Avon. On the right are the timber-framed Almshouses built by the Guild of the Holy Cross in the first half of the 14th century and still giving homes for 24 elderly people. The Guild's Chapel with its tower is in the centre of the picture overshadowing the site of Shakespeare's New Place with the Guildhall (and the Grammar School above it) joining the Almshouses to the Chapel to complete one of the longest Tudor facades in England.

The Great Garden of New Place, Stratford-on-Avon. This is, of course, the new 'New Place' because the great tragedy of Stratford is that Shakespeare's New Place where he spent his closing years and died at the early age of 52, was demolished by the Rev Francis Gastrell in 1759. Resenting the intrusion of visitors upon his privacy, he first cut down Shakespeare's famous mulberry tree and three years later destroyed the house. The Great Garden depicted here covers the land behind Shakespeare's house which was cultivated in his day as a kitchen garden and an orchard. It is now maintained as a memorial to him by the Birthplace Trust. The house in the background is Nash's House which, though refronted in modern times, was there in Shakespeare's day and now houses the New Place Museum. On the left of the picture is the Guild Chapel which was founded in 1269. Its fabric is now deteriorating but, thanks to the efforts of the Association of Friends of Guild Chapel, it is being gradually restored.

Harvard House, High Street, Stratford-on-Avon. Harvard House was new when Shakespeare returned to live in Stratford — it was built in 1596. The daughter of its first owners, Thomas and Alice Rogers, whose initials and the date appear under the first storey window, married Robert Harvard and their son John, born in 1607, emigrated to America. He died in 1638 leaving '£779 17s 2d' together with his library of over 300 books, for the founding of Harvard College. The 'Ancient House' as it was then known, gradually fell into decay until the novelist Marie Corelli, who did much to restore Stratford, persuaded Mr E. Morris of Chicago to buy the house in 1909. He presented it to Harvard College and a board of Trustees appointed by the College still administers it. During World War II it was used as a club by thousands of American servicemen.

Anne Hathaway's Cottage, Shottery, Stratford-on-Avon. Warwickshire thatch with 'crucks' to support it, wattle and daub, some brick panels and a central chimney stack built 80 years after Shakespeare's death all make up the home of the Hathaway family from 1470 to 1911. It is perhaps the most famous house in England and the epitome of what many believe a cottage in the country should be. Shakespeare married Anne in 1582 and over many years loving care has been lavished on this cottage that was her parental home to restore it to that period. It contains many items from Shakespeare's day — a 'courting' settle, a giant carved Elizabethan bedstead that has been in the same room for 400 years, and many homely implements of dairy and kitchen. Especially attractive is the garden:

'I know a bank where the wild tyme blows,
Where oxslips and the nodding violet grows'

Lord Leycester's Hospital, Warwick. Standing on a terrace above Warwick's Old West Gate, Lord Leycester's Hospital which was founded in 1571 commands a fine view across Warwick racecourse to the Cotswold Hills. Just as the name of its founder retains its medieval spelling so the word 'hospital' retains its original meaning and purpose. It offers hospitality — not treatment — to 12 men or 'Brethren' 'hurt in the wars' and their wives as it has done for over 400 years. Twelve ex-Servicemen drawn from all three Services and their wives have apartments here and the men, wearing Elizabethan style hats, cloaks and scarves, act as guides to visitors. The 'jettied' building itself was built by the United Guilds of Warwick in the 14th century and one reason offered for its survival is the use of Spanish chestnut for its roof frames. (Observe the Warwickshire badge of 'bear and ragged staff' over the doorway.) The gateway is tunnelled through solid sandstone rock and the diminutive chapel above it is dedicated to St James and was built in 1123.

Oken's House, Warwick. Thomas Oken, a poor Warwick boy in Tudor times, acquired a vast fortune as a merchant and mercer and bequeathed it with his house, shown here, to the town in 1573. The house which has been carefully restored is now the home of the Warwick Doll Museum, an interesting collection of many kinds of dolls of all types — wood, china, metal, and wax — and dressed in the costume of many ages.

Bridge End and Castle, Warwick. A disastrous fire in 1694 burned down more than 250 houses in Warwick but happily left many groups of gabled, timber-framed and brick-nogged houses like the terrace in the picture. Behind stands the imposing mass of Warwick Castle which Sir Walter Scott described as: 'the fairest monument of ancient and chivalrous splendour which yet remains uninjured by time.' The tower on the left is Caesar's Tower, 147ft high; that on the right is Guy's Tower completed in 1394 and 128ft high. Between the two towers is the gatehouse and Barbican. Until very recently the castle was still owned by the Earls of Warwick — the Greville family — and was renowned for its collection of armour and of pictures. It is now owned by Madame Tussauds.

The Windmill, Chesterton, Warwickshire. Perched on a hilltop alongside the old Fosse Way and overlooking the site of a Roman staging camp, this unusual windmill was originally built as an astronomical observatory for the local landowner, Sir Edward Peyto, in 1642. Its designer was the outstanding English architect Inigo Jones who introduced the Palladian style to this country and was responsible for many outstanding buildings of the early Stuart period including the Banqueting Hall in Whitehall and the Queen's House at Greenwich.

Stubble Burning, north of Shipston-on-Stour, Warwickshire. A reminder that although it contains the great Midlands conurbation of Birmingham and Coventry, Warwickshire is nonetheless primarily an agricultural county — and the home, at Stoneleigh, of the 'Royal', Britain's premier agricultural show. The Stour valley which runs from the Cotswold edge to the Avon south of Stratford is a particularly fertile area. The burning of stubble which is now widespread in England is claimed by some to help check pests and insects and increase soil fertility. Others fear the damage it does to wild-life — including the fast-disappearing partridge — by destroying the winter's 'gleaning'.

Chastleton House, near Moreton-in-Marsh, Oxfordshire. A superb example of the Jacobean style of manor house, Chastleton House was built in 1603 by Walter Jones. It is virtually unchanged since it was built and an inventory in the house taken in 1633 shows that much of its original furniture also survives. It has associations with Robert Catesby, one of the Gunpowder Plot conspirators, and also contains one of the secret rooms frequently found in houses of this period. In 1651 the room was responsible for saving the life of its then owner, Arthur Jones, who had galloped home from the battle of Worcester where he had fought on the losing Royalist side. Cromwell's soldiers were close behind and although they searched Chastleton and interrogated Mrs Jones, they failed to find him. She drugged their wine and while they slept, Jones escaped.

CHASTLETON HOUSE
open weekdays
(closed Wednesdays)
10·30 a.m–1pm 2·4·30 pm
or dusk in winter
Sunday 2–5pm
Admission 60p Children 30p
Gardens only 10p

Stow-on-the-Wold, Gloucestershire. 'Stow-on-the-Wold-where-the-wind-blows-cold' is the highest town in the Cotswolds on a hilltop nearly 800ft high between the valleys of Dikler and the Evenlode. All roads in Gloucestershire seem to lead to Stow and it was for centuries the busiest market in the Cotswolds. Daniel Defoe, writing in the early 1700s, tells of 20,000 sheep being sold in Stow's market. It has a time-honoured role as a resting place for the refreshment of travellers of all kinds — the King's Arms here, for example, has been an inn since 1647 and was known as the best staging post between London and Worcester. Nowadays Stow is perhaps best known for its two horse fairs held in May and October each year. It was also involved in the last battle of the first Civil War — the actual site is between Donnington and Stow — and several hundred Royalist prisoners were confined in St Edward's Church after they surrendered to the Cromwellians. A fascinating collection of Civil War relics is to be found in the museum in the Town Hall including contemporary portraits by Van Dyck.

Upper Slaughter, Gloucestershire. This charming Cotswold village and its downstream neighbour – Lower Slaughter – are in the valley of the tiny River Eye which joins the Dikler on its way into the Windrush and on to the Thames. Happily the name 'Slaughter' has nothing to do with bloodshed, battle or strife which have been remote from these peaceful villages since time immemorial. One explanation for the name is that it is derived from an Old English word *slohtre* meaning a slough or muddy place and only too appropriate in winter to both villages. Another explanation is that the name derives from the Anglo-Saxon for sloe-tree – Slaughter being a place of the sloes. Certainly there are plenty of sloes to be found locally.

50

Lower Slaughter, Gloucestershire. Both villages are much beloved by painters – and photographers – and these cottages are one of the reasons. Steep-gabled, stone-walled, they are superb examples of the Cotswold tradition of domestic architecture in its most homely form.

Bourton-on-the-Water, Gloucester. Sited close to the bridge where the Fosse crosses the Windrush, Bourton-on-the-Water has been settled since Roman times. On Fosse Way there was once a Roman staging post and a few years ago one of the few Saxon dwellings that have survived in England was found on the edge of the village. In keeping with the long-standing Cotswold tradition, it appears to have been the home of a weaver. The Windrush flows alongside the road through the middle of the village and is crossed by these graceful low stone footbridges dating back to 1756. Another of Bourton's celebrated attractions in the yard of the old New Inn is an accurate model of the village one-tenth in scale that contains a model of itself, that contains a model of . . . .

54

Little Barrington, Near Burford, Gloucester-shire. These ancient cottages at Little Barrington are set along the rim of a grass-covered bowl that was once the quarry from which the stones that built them were dug. Notice the tiny Gothic arch in the middle of the row with its characteristic stone-drip. The stone for this village and its counter-part, Great Barrington, on the other side of the Windrush, as well as for the great house, Barrington Park, came from these local quarries. And the masons who built them reared here too.

The High Street, Burford, Oxfordshire. Burford is one of the gateways to the Cotswolds and has a thousand years of history behind it. As its name implies, it was originally built up around a ford across the Windrush and it greatly prospered from the wool trade. With the discovery of good quality building stone in the vicinity of Barrington, wooden framed buildings — Burford was once surrounded by the forest of Wychwood — were replaced by Cotswold stone ones and the appearance of the town is little changed from that of the 17th century — apart, that is, for the cars. Charles II was a frequent visitor after the Restoration and Nell Gwynne was particularly fond of it.

At her insistence, her eldest son was given the title of Earl of Burford. She threatened to throw the baby out of a window unless the King granted her wish.

Little Faringdon Mill, Near Lechlade, Oxfordshire. On the very edge of the Cotswolds, this stone millhouse is on the River Leach which rises in the hills close to Hampnett and gives its name to Northleach near its source and Lechlade close to where it joins the Thames. For the harmony of mellow stone reflected in tranquil water there are few places to equal Little Faringdon Mill, even in the Cotswolds.

Lechlade, Gloucestershire. More mellow stone reflected in tranquil water but the water this time is the Thames, a busy throughfare now for pleasure craft of all kinds; in earlier times famous for its barge traffic. Barges used to queue here to enter the now derelict Thames-Severn Canal at Inglesham, half a mile upstream. The Cotswold stones for the dome of St Paul's Cathedral were loaded on barges here, for example, but the main trade was in salt. Salt dug in Droitwich was carried by pack-horse down the Salt Way across the Cotswolds and loaded here for London.

Arlington Row, Bibury, Gloucestershire. Perhaps the most famous row of cottages in England and possibly the most beautiful. These cottages earned from William Morris, the 19th century poet and artist and the first to recognise and appreciate the 'Cotswold vernacular', the accolade that Bibury was 'the most beautiful village in England'. They are built of local stone and probably date from the early 17th century, and were then occupied by weavers who served the local fulling mill.

The Market Place, Cirencester. Cirencester – pronounced nowadays as it is spelt – has strong claims to being the capital of the Cotswolds. Founded in AD50 by the Romans and then called Corinium Dobunnorum, it stands at the crossroads of five major roads and is the focal point of many more ancient tracks and bridleways. The market place is dominated by the Parish Church of St John the Baptist whose tower and south porch are shown here. The tower was built between 1400 and 1450 and was originally intended to have a spire. The porch was added about 1490 and after the Dissolution served for a time as Town Hall. It was rebuilt in the 19th century and a number of old houses adjoining it were demolished to be replaced by the Georgian

houses seen on the right. One of the tower's statues is of the patron saint – St John the Baptist – and has become blackened with time hence the irreverent name of the street it overlooks – 'Blackjack Street'.

The Ford, Duntisbourne Leer, Gloucestershire. About three miles outside Cirencester
just off the Roman road to Gloucester,
Duntisbourne Leer takes its name from two
sources — first it is on the charming little river
Dun a tributary of the Churn; second, it once
belonged to the Abbey of Lire in Normandy.

South Porch, Malmesbury Abbey Church, Malmesbury, Wiltshire. A place of pilgrimage since the earliest days of Christianity in Britain – there is said to have been a convent here in the 6th century – Malmesbury Abbey once contained among its treasures a piece of the True Cross, a Thorn from the Crown of Thorns and the bones of St Aldhelm, an early English saint who died in 705. After the Dissolution the Abbey, apart from the nave which became the parish church, was allowed to fall into decay and no attempts at repair or restoration were made until 1823. Happily the magnificent South Porch seen here has survived with its richly carved entrance arches remarkably preserved. They are generally regarded as the finest example of Norman decorative stonework in Britain. There is a legend that in the year 1010 when Malmesbury Abbey had a tower, a monk called Oliver made himself a pair of wings and cheerfully jumped from the top. He was badly crippled but lived to tell his tale. As the tower was more than 120ft high, he must have come close to becoming the first Englishman ever to fly.

The Market Cross, Castle Coombe, Wiltshire. Stone-built and stone-tiled and very much in the Cotswold vernacular style, this market cross is one of the delights of a village that retains a great deal of its original Tudor character and has been voted the prettiest village in England. Until the 15th century, markets — especially wool and cloth markets common in the Cotswolds — were held in the nave of the local church on Sundays. (Usually the church was the only building big enough and Sunday the only day that people could attend.) Gradually the markets were forced out of the nave to the porch, then to the churchyard and finally into the street leading to the church. So that the buyers and sellers should not forget that though they were no longer in church and the day was now Saturday, the market was still in God's name, market crosses were built in the more important market towns. Later on these simple crosses were extended to include shelter for booths and the Church levied a rent. This market cross is a reminder that in former times Castle Coombe was an important commercial centre for the wool trade in the south Cotswolds.

Beverstone Castle, near Tetbury, Gloucestershire. The remains of the castle date from c1225 but there was a castle on the site before the Normans came and King Harold stayed here in 1051. The castle, then much more formidable than it is now, was besieged twice during the Civil War by the Parliamentarians. It was only captured the second time because its governor, Colonel Oglethorpe, was taken prisoner while courting a young woman at a neighbouring farm. He was then forced to reveal the castle's weak points. The house which occupies the site of the 13th century hall has been altered several times. After being damaged by fire in 1691 the roof was replaced and it seems likely that the mullioned and transomed windows date from the same time.

Upton House, Tetbury Upton, Gloucester-shire. An elegant 18th century house in an elegant village, Upton House was built for Thomas Cripps in 1752. It is stone-built in a type of masonry known as 'ashlar' — indenti-fiable from its smooth finished face, accur-ately shaped blocks and thin joints. Note the rusticated (ie grooved) quoins, the dentil cornice and the balustraded parapet. This is hardly Cotswold vernacular but indubitably Cotswold stone at its radiant best.

76

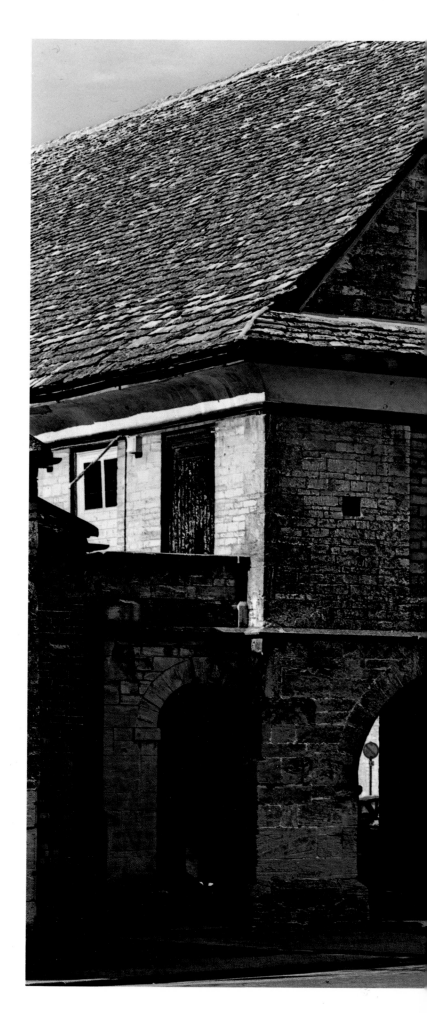

Market House, Minchinhampton, Gloucestershire. Another Cotswold wool and cloth town, Minchinhampton was also a centre for the quarrying of good quality stone — a fact which is reflected here in the walls and roofing of both the Market Hall which dates from 1698 and the splendid Crown Inn with its nine sash windows. Minchinhampton is also known for the golf course on its celebrated Common where quarries serve as bunkers. The town is also close to Gatcombe Park, an ashlar-faced 18th century mansion originally built for Edward Sheppard, a rich clothier. It has since been owned by David Ricardo, the political economist and Lord Butler. It is now the home of Princess Anne.

Owlpen Manor, Uley, Gloucestershire. A gentle tree-lined stream, wooded hillside, a sheep-filled pasture and a mellow stone church and manor house complete with corn mill and massive barn — the epitome of the south Cotswold hamlet, as it has been since medieval times. The church is 19th century but the Manor House in classic Cotswold-style gables, stone roof, mullioned windows with dripmoulds, tall chimneys, carved finials — is Elizabethan in origin. The gazebo or garden room on the left of the house is late 17th century. Owlpen Manor was unoccupied from about 1850 to 1926 when an architect, Norman Jewson, bought the house and restored it.

Landscape between Uley and Dursley, Gloucestershire. The B4066 road from Dursley through Uley to the Stroud Valley is one of the most spectacular in the Cotswold area running as it does along the steep south western escarpment overlooking the Vale of Berkeley and the upper estuary of the Severn. The hill in the background is Downham Hill – an island hill known locally as Smallpox Hill as it once housed an isolation hospital for smallpox victims. Uley and Dursley were centres of the wool weaving industry and Uley blue cloth was renowned throughout Europe. In earlier times much of it was produced in isolated houses like the one shown here. Dursley remains a major centre for the production of 'West of England' cloth.

Bisley, near Stroud, Gloucestershire. Set in the hills above the upper Frome's 'Golden Valley' — so called because of its colours especially in autumn, not its wealth — Bisley is another gem-like Cotswold stone village in a golden setting. Wesley House, shown here, is in the Cotswold vernacular and has features identified with the 16th, 17th and 18th centuries. Its connexion with John Wesley dates back to the early 1740s when Wesley made many preaching expeditions into the Cotswolds from his headquarters in Bristol. The walls of the house are rubble with ashlar quoins and the oval attic window is often found in houses in the traditional style.

Painswick Churchyard, Painswick, Gloucestershire.

*'Beggarly Bisley, Strutting Stroud,
Mincing Hampton and Painswick Proud'*

Painswick has many things to be proud of. It was in at the beginning of the clothing trade when a colony of Flemish weavers settled in the town in the 16th century. It prospered and grew over the centuries and much of its prosperity is evident today in the splendid size and character of its houses. Its church too has a proud history and still carries on its walls the marks of flame and shot from the Civil War. But perhaps Painswick's proudest possession is its churchyard with its 99 ancient yew trees planted c1792 — there is a legend that no one ever counts the same number twice — and its tombs, many of them table-topped as seen here. The style of the table-topped tombs is Renaissance — a style which did not reach the area until the 18th century. The carving was carried out by local masons and some of them are buried under similar tombs in this churchyard.

The Devil's Chimney, Leckhampton Hill, near Cheltenham, Gloucestershire. This prominent landmark alongside the B4070 between Cheltenham and Birdlip is not a natural formation nor does it owe its origin to Infernal help. It is most probably a quarryman's joke dating from about 1790 when Leckhampton Hill was actively quarried. Its most likely origin was as a wedge-shaped peninsula created when a light railway was cut diagonally up the face of the quarry. Quarrymen then helped with both the shaping and the creation of the legend that it was the Devil's work. Made of 'freestone' — notice the regular and horizontal bedding — it is already eroding rapidly especially on the western side and the effect of frost is opening the natural joints in the rock. Without suitable reinforcement it seems unlikely to survive for more than a decade or two.

The Promenade, Cheltenham, Gloucestershire. Cheltenham's claim to be a Cotswold town goes back far beyond the mere 200 years since the chance discovery of its curative waters in 1761 brought it into prominence as a spa. It began life as a market town serving the farms and villages over a wide area — a role it still fulfils today under a more modern guise as shopping centre. But there is no escaping the legacy of its more genteel past. It still gives the visitor a sense of past elegance, civilised planning and a rare feeling of civic dignity and pride. No better example could be found than the spaciousness of The Promenade and this adjoining Regency terrace now serving as what must be the most stylish municipal offices in the country. It is faced with Cotswold stone from Leckhampton.

Cotswold Countryside — looking east from Belas Knap near Winchcombe. Typical Cotswold landscape of the north-west corner — the top of the escarpment where the land rises to almost 1,000ft. Belas Knap itself is a carefully preserved example of a Stone Age burial mound dating from about 1400BC sited close to a hilltop on the route of the ancient Cotswold Ridgeway which runs from just outside Bath to Broadway Hill. It is part of one of the great trackways from the Avon to the Humber that kept to the hilltops and avoided the dangers of the wooded valleys in prehistoric times. The view here is of the valley of the little river Isborne which runs through Winchcombe to Evesham where it joins the Avon. Along the top of the opposite ridge runs the Saltway — the pack-horse track that carried salt from Droitwich to Lechlade where it was loaded into boats for London.

Cutsdean, Gloucestershire. Cutsdean is the site of the spring which forms the source of the river Windrush, the largest of the Cotswold rivers. The village itself is 750ft above sea-level while Cutsdean Hill rises to 1,001ft. It would be difficult to find a more 'typical' north Cotswold hamlet or one where the Cotswold stone of its buildings blends more harmoniously into the Cotswold landscape.

The Gatehouse, Stanway, near Toddington, Gloucestershire. Stanway nestles under the Cotswold escarpment where an ancient road — Stane, or stone, Way — climbed up into the hills. Stanway House was built in Elizabethan and Stuart times by the Tracy family and this gatehouse was probably built about 1630. The three shaped gables are surmounted by scallop shells, the emblem of the Tracy family, and they also appear over the pediment of the doorway and as finials. Note the deep colour of the stone, a characteristic of deep quarried stone known as Yellow Guiting stone after the Guiting Power quarry. It is found in many buildings in the area.

Stanway Park, Stanway, Gloucestershire. At all times of the year the quiet little road which runs along the foot of the escarpment between Stanway and Stanton is full of colour and charm from the bright gold of springtime laburnum to the russet of autumn oak. Here in the evening sunlight, sheep graze under the oak trees of the parkland surrounding the great house of Stanway.

Stanton, near Broadway, Gloucestershire. Stanton is a twin village to Stanway and architecturally it is one of the most distinguished of the northern Cotswolds. Most of its houses carry dates c1615 when the yeoman of the district were at their most prosperous and when the Cotswold tradition in building was at its peak. Practically every variation can be found in Stanton. Much of the credit for the careful preservation of the village is due to one of its former owners, Sir Philip Stott, an architect who bought the Stanton estate in 1906. Before he died in 1936 he also built a reservoir and a swimming pool in the valley above the village.

Snowshill Manor, Snowshill, Gloucester-shire. This manor house, now owned by the National Trust, was built around 1500 and has been altered several times since. The manor itself was originally given to the Abbot of Winchcombe by Kenulf, King of the Saxon kingdom of Mercia, in 821. At the Dissolution King Henry VIII gave it to his wife, Katherine Parr. Although it is another superb example of the Cotswold idiom in architectural style, the main interest is not so much in the house as in its contents. From 1919 until 1951 when he handed it over to the Trust, Snowshill was owned by an eccentric collector, Charles Wade, who devoted his fortune to acquiring an incredible accumulation of strange and unusual objects. The Trust has kept the collection intact and it is all still to be seen – Jacobean furniture, old compasses, telescopes, ship models, musical instruments, boneshaker bicycles, even Japanese armour and Persian lamps – a veritable magpie's Aladdin's Cave.

The Churchyard, Snowshill, Gloucestershire. On the very edge of the escarpment under the appropriately named Oat Hill, seen here in the background, Snowshill was frequently isolated in bad weather in earlier times and even today has a feeling of self-preserving compactness about it. There has been a settlement on this site for thousands of years — the British Museum has a dagger and pin from the Bronze Age and an axe from the Stone Age that were found locally. The church of St Barnabas, seen here, was built in 1864 on the site of an earlier Norman church of which only the font and pulpit remain.

Cotswold landscape near Temple Guiting, Gloucestershire. The heart of the Cotswolds — gentle rolling hills, open skies, old woods and ancient trees, even older stone-walls, reddish soil and the golden stubble of autumn.

106

Sunset over Broadway and the Vale of
Evesham. In this remarkable photograph
taken from the upper slopes of Willersey
Hill it is possible to pick out the silhouette
of the Malvern hills and, nearer, the profile
of the northern slopes of Bredon Hill. In the
middle ground is the double crown of
Blakes Hill and the villages of Aston
108 Somerville and Childswickham.

Broadway Tower, Broadway Beacon. The story goes that the Countess of Coventry whose husband owned Broadway Beacon at the end of the 17th century, had a bonfire lit here to discover whether or not it could be seen from the family seat, Crome Court, near Worcester, some 25 miles away. The fire was clearly seen and the Countess persuaded the Earl to build a tower. The work was completed in 1797 and from the top of the tower on a clear day it is possible to pick out the Black Mountains of Wales, the Malverns, Worcester Cathedral, the spires of Coventry and the roofs of Shakespeare's Stratford. It was used as an artist's retreat in the 19th century by three painters of the pre-Raphaelite school, William Morris, Rossetti and Burne Jones. It is now a museum and open to the public.

Bibliography

Cotswolds and the Shakespeare Country; Ed J. W. Hammond (RedGuide) Ward Lock
Portrait of the Cotswolds; Edith Brill, Robert Hale
Geology Explained in the Severn Vale and Cotswolds; W. Dreghorn, David & Charles
The Folklore of the Cotswolds; Katherine M. Briggs, Batsford
Warwickshire; Vivian Bird, Batsford
The King's England: *Gloucestershire*; Arthur Mee, Hodder & Stoughton
The King's England: *Worcestershire*; Arthur Mee, Hodder & Stoughton
The King's England: *Warwickshire*; Arthur Mee, Hodder & Stoughton
The Buildings of England, Ed Nicklaus Pevsner: *Gloucestershire and the Cotswolds*; David Verey, Penguin Books
The Making of the English Landscape: *The Gloucestershire Landscape;* H. P. R. Finberg, Hodder & Stoughton